Fathers

The *best* is *yet to be*

GEORGE and SEDENA
CAPPANNELLI

How to age wisely and fall in love with your life...**AGAIN**!

simple truths®
Your Destination For Inspiration
an imprint of Sourcebooks, Inc.

Editing by: Alice Patenaude

Photo Credits
Cover: front, Elena Kalistratova/Thinkstock; back, Krivosheev Vitaly/Shutterstock
Internals: page 1, Elena Kalistratova/Thinkstock; pages 2–3, Scorpp/Shutterstock; pages 4–5, Elenamiv/Shutterstock; page 6, Kesu/Shutterstock; page 8, LilKar/Shutterstock; pages 10–11, Elenamiv/Shutterstock; pages 14–15, kosmos111/Shutterstock; pages 16–17, MiAdS/Shutterstock; pages 18–19, Elenamiv/Shutterstock; page 21, Dave Allen Photography/Shutterstock; pages 24–25, anawat sudchanham/Shutterstock; page 28, archideaphoto/Shutterstock; pages 30–31, maigi/Shutterstock; pages 38–39, sellingpix/Thinkstock; pages 44–45, DC_Colombia/Thinkstock; page 49, the-P-A-N-O-R-A-M-A-studio/Thinkstock; pages 50–51, Elenamiv/Shutterstock; page 55, MariuszBlach/Thinkstock; pages 58–59, Jo Ann Snover/Shutterstock; pages 64–65, Mike_Pellinni/Thinkstock; page 69, Patrizia Tilly/Shutterstock; page 71, varuna/Shutterstock; pages 72–73, Efired/Shutterstock; pages 78–79, Iakov Kalinin/Shutterstock; page 84, Relix Image/Shutterstock; pages 92–93, ehrlif/Thinkstock; page 99, maryTR/Thinkstock; pages 100–101, Jessmine/Shutterstock; page 106, Givaga/Thinkstock; pages 114–115, Creative Travel Projects/Shutterstock; page 121, narloch-liberra/Thinkstock; pages 122–123, Frank Fennema/Shutterstock; page 129, sborisov/Thinkstock; pages 130–131, Dudarev Mikhail/Shutterstock; pages 136–137, Nelepl/Thinkstock; page 141, keanu2/Thinkstock

Published by Simple Truths, an imprint of Sourcebooks, Inc.
P.O. Box 4410, Naperville, Illinois 60567-4410
(630) 961-3900
Fax: (630) 961-2168
www.sourcebooks.com

Originally published in 2013 in the United States by AMI/AgeNation/Hay House.

Printed and bound in the United States of America.
WOZ 10 9 8 7 6 5 4 3 2 1

INTRODUCTION

The Gift

One day, as we in haste rushed
along the road well-traveled, we
saw ahead an old and stooped figure
walking with a slow and labored tread.
Anxious for our destination and tired
from years spent traveling on the road, we
were, at first, inclined to pass the figure by.

*But when we came abreast, an old
and friendly face turned in our direction.
And what we saw in his clear
and vibrant eyes
made us slow our pace
and pause just long enough to ask
if we might aid him in some way.*

He smiled; kindness and something more we could not at first name were present in his eyes. "No," he said. "But thank you for your kindness. And if you are inclined to linger with me awhile, I have a gift I will share with you. For it is clear your hearts are true."

For a few instants or maybe longer,
impatience whispered gruffly in our ears.
"Move on!" it said. "You have no time to dally.
This old one will only slow you down." But
another voice, softer, but with a most compelling
sound, spoke. "Stay awhile," it said. "There
is always time enough for truth and kindness."

So we smiled at the old one, who, in turn,
gestured to a shady grove beside the road
where we sat upon a soft and friendly ground.
For a while, however, he did not speak,
but in those clear and vibrant eyes, there was
a sense of quiet and something more,
something that felt very familiar.

"The gift," he said, "is this. No matter
what road you take, there are secrets that
will, if you hold them close and practice them true,
guide you surely to your destination. And while those
who search for shiny things, promises of gold and
names renown, place little value on them,
I tell you this: real gold lies within their folds."

He paused again. His deep and quiet gaze resting gently on us. Yet it seemed as though he was not just looking at but deep within us, to that place where we held our secrets, including our hunger for shiny things, promises of gold and names renowned. We were, in fact, concerned he would see this hunger and withdraw his offer.

After what seemed an almost endless wait, he nodded slowly several times and began to speak. It was then we felt ourselves release a breath so deep it seemed we had been holding it all our lives. And in that moment we understood the time had indeed come for us to receive the gift this traveler had for us.

*The old one's voice had a unique timbre
and cadence that drew us to him,
the sound resonant and deep,
and yet it placed no demand upon us.
It did, however, contain a strong sense
of the road, of many miles traveled
and many things seen.*

"To live life fully," he said, "I have found it valuable to remember that life is a journey of discovery during which I am constantly given the opportunity to live more consciously and age wisely. And I do this best when I remember I did not come into this life to dance to someone else's tune or meet someone else's expectations.

"My task instead is to live the life that I, and I alone, am born to live." With this the old one took a well-worn manuscript from his pack. He held it fondly for a moment before extending it to us. "This I leave in your care while I do something I must do. But I will return." He left us then and we, in turn, carefully opened the cover and began to read.

In the
Beginning

"Everything has to do with
loving and not loving."

—RUMI

This is a time of demographic revolution. Over the next several decades, a large number—some say half of our population—will be fifty years of age or older for the first time in history. Although this revolution is still in its early stages, it is clear from the conversations and conflicts being acted out in the chambers of government and in the boardrooms of our institutions and corporations that this "graying" of the world's population is ushering in a time of unprecedented social, political, cultural, economic, technological, and environmental change. This is true for all who are passengers on this train called humanity, and especially for those of us who are older—Gen Xers (thirties and forties), Boomers (fifty to sixty-eight), and Elders (sixty-eight-plus), and for younger people who seek to live more consciously and who will soon inherit full responsibility for the future. And this, as they say, is only the beginning!

Couple this reality with the knowledge that these governments, institutions, businesses, and the vast majority of us are unprepared for these substantial challenges and unprecedented opportunities, and it is easy to understand how this confluence of factors can be either a recipe for disaster or fertile ground for a historic breakthrough.

The message in these pages weighs in on the side of fertile ground for breakthrough. Gen Xers, Boomers, and Elders have the opportunity, time, resources, talent, experience, and need to revisit our values and priorities and squeeze the juice from this fruit of our experience.

We can contribute to charting a new course for the future that will be healthier, saner, more sustainable, and more constructive for ourselves and those who come after us.

So if you fall within one of these demographic groups and are interested in living more consciously and aging wisely, you are, as they say, on the right page at the right time. If you are under forty and want to better prepare for your own road ahead—as well as better understand the road your parents, older friends, and relatives are now on—then you have also come to the right place.

If you want to use the time you have remaining—whether years or decades—to make right your relationship with yourself and with others, if you want to connect with greater meaning, passion, and contribute to a more positive and compassionate future, then the words on these pages are for you.

They have been written to remind us all to use this precious gift of life to turn the fruits of our past into gold to invest in the present and future. For only by living in each present moment with greater mindfulness and by answering the fundamental question each of us will face at the end of our lives—*Have I best used my time, skills, resources, and heart to lead a life of genuine value?*—can we fulfill the dream we have come here to manifest.

Life Rule

"But it is too late for me, you might say, I am already full-grown. Not so, for in the world of our inwardness, we are always growing... We can return and begin again by facing ourselves. In this way, we can go below our hardened ways to the soft impulses that birth them. Instead of breaking the bone of our stubbornness, we can nourish the marrow of our feeling unheard... Instead of counting the scars from being hurt in the world, we can find and re-kiss the very spot in our soul where we began to withhold our trust."

—MARK NEPO

PART ONE

As It Is Now

"There lies before us, if we choose, continual progress in happiness, knowledge, and wisdom… We appeal as human beings to human beings: Remember your humanity, and forget the rest. If you can do so, the way lies open to a new Paradise…"

—BERTRAND RUSSELL AND ALBERT EINSTEIN

Do Not Go Quietly

"What we reach for may be different,
but what makes us reach is the same."

—MARK NEPO

An Invitation to Conscious Living and Wise Aging

This chapter, indeed this small book, takes its inspiration in part from Dylan Thomas's well-loved poem "Do Not Go Gentle into That Good Night." The opening stanza of his poem reads:

> *Do not go gentle into that good night,*
> *Old age should burn and rave at close of day;*
> *Rage, rage against the dying of the light.*

"Old age should burn and rave at close of day." What a line! What a powerful and essential message for this time of demographic shift.

Dylan Thomas wrote these words to express his regret and frustration over his father's diminishing capacities, limited resources, and unfulfilled promises, as well as some of his own unfinished dreams. These are things all of us encounter some of the time and some of us encounter a lot of the time during the second half of life, and yet, rather than be saddened or troubled by these lines, you are invited to hear them as a call to action, as a reminder to take full advantage of the time remaining in your life. And to wisely do with this time what your heart knows will allow you to complete your journey with dignity, originality, and honor.

Instead of regret, let these lines encourage you to let your passion burn and lead you into a deeper inquiry into why you are here and what you still have left to discover. Let them guide you to honor and celebrate all of the stages of life, even—and particularly—the last. Without this honoring, you run the risk of arriving at the end of your journey having missed important opportunities and essential lessons that contribute to a life of greater meaning and purpose.

So let us make a collective declaration of faith and hope that each of us who are a part of this second half of life contingent—which will eventually number 150 million Americans, and billions more around the planet—will not fade meekly and invisibly into the background. Instead, we will step more fully into our lives with true compassion for ourselves and for those who may have lost their way so that we can leave behind a legacy of promise and not one of regret.

Let us not fritter away the time we have remaining but instead let us model a new vitality and integrity, one that does not value physical accomplishments, material possessions, or financial wealth exclusively and above the quality of our character and the amount of compassion, consciousness, and love we express in our every interaction.

Let us listen as much to our hearts as our heads, commit to a deeper level of healing for ourselves and those we love, participate in the future with more grace and compassion, and connect more deeply with our dream so that we can joyfully sing our unique notes in the "great song of life."

Life Rule

"Young. Old. Just words."
—GEORGE BURNS

Life Achievement

Jeanne-Louise Calment lived 122 years and 164 days. She lived longer than any other person thus far documented. Jeanne was still riding her bicycle at 100 years of age.

Life Tool

There is one rule to value above many others: "To thine own self be true." Consider ways in which you can be truer to yourself today. What can you do to express more of what is authentic and original within you so that you can contribute to making your own life—and the lives of those around you—more joyful, engaging, and rewarding?

Lifestyle
Revolution

"We are members of a vast, cosmic orchestra in which each living instrument is essential to the complementary and harmonious playing of the whole."

—J. ALLEN BOONE

This Brave New World

One of the most daunting and exciting aspects of this dawning demographic revolution is that the world of the future, especially for those of us who are in the second half of life, will not be just incrementally but radically different from the world into which we were born, matured, had families, and participated in careers from which unprecedented numbers of us are now retiring—either by our choice or that of others.

Kelly Greene, former staff reporter for the *Wall Street Journal*, described aspects of this new world this way: "The baby boom is about to enter its golden years—and getting older will never be the same. Cell phones that monitor your body temperature and sleep patterns. Cruise ships that take the place of retirement communities. 'Brain gyms' where you sharpen your wits with computer games. Video autobiographies and interactive cemeteries. And this is only the beginning."

What else are futurists saying about this brave new world? Longevity will increase to an average age of 120. Our profit-based healthcare system, the only remaining holdout in the entire industrial world, will implode under the weight of increasing numbers and skyrocketing costs. Meals in a pill will become the rule of the day.

Fully computerized and automated forms of transportation, homes, and commercial buildings will become standard.

Others predict a united global economy, fully automated robotic manufacturing communities, time travel, space communities, telepathy, bubble cities, underwater cities, and much more. And these extraordinary changes, as far-fetched as some seem, will only be the beginning.

The Part We Can Play

In the face of these changes, those of us in the second half of life will, out of necessity, find ourselves needing to play a more engaged role in influencing the course our world takes, at least if we want to protect the quality of our lives. Older Gen Xers, Boomers, and Elders have a vital role to play in turning the ship in a more meaningful direction.

In the United States, Boomers and Elders control a very significant percentage of our nation's financial assets. They account for a significant amount of discretionary spending in the United States, including personal care products, apparel, and particularly new cars. They also are responsible for the largest percentage of the leisure travel dollars and, as one would imagine, the lion's share of healthcare spending, doling out more on healthcare insurance than any other single demographic group.

Yes, those of us in the second half of life have the power to make a real difference, but only if we commit to putting our own houses in order first and exercise our true power by living consciously and aging wisely.

We can initiate another lifestyle revolution in which we reclaim our sovereignty, redefine our priorities, redirect our resources, honor our wisdom and experience, and contribute our significant array of gifts and talents to a society badly in need of them. To do this, we will, of course, have to set aside our obsession with youth and reclaim our rightful place as the keepers and transmitters of wisdom.

Life Rule

"The secret to living a successful life lies in the practice and mastery of the basics."
—ANONYMOUS

Life Achievements

Dame Judi Dench, one of the world's most acclaimed actresses, is nearing eighty and continues to astound and delight audiences around the world.

Life Tool

Ask yourself: "Is my life in balance or out of balance?" If your answer is that your life is out of balance, you might want to identify what aspects of your life need attention—career, relationships, spiritual practice, pursuit of your personal dream, education, or your contribution to the world around you. Then, identify at least one specific thing you can do in each area to regain and better maintain your balance.

PART TWO

Questions &
Encouragements
for the Road Ahead

"To be joyful in the universe is a brave and reckless act. The courage for joy springs not from the certainty of human experience, but the surprise... Therefore, despite the world's sorrows, we give thanks for our loves, for our joys, and for the continued courage to be happily surprised."

—MOLLY FUMIA

The Ruts of Ordinary Perception

"To be shaken out of the ruts of ordinary perception, to be shown for a few timeless hours the outer and inner world, not as they appear to [one]… obsessed with words and notions, but as they are apprehended, directly and unconditionally, by [our souls]—this is an experience of inestimable value…"

—ALDOUS HUXLEY

Time and Perception

"To be shaken out of the ruts of ordinary perception." Is it possible? Aldous Huxley thought it was. So have other pioneers who have experimented with the boundaries of human consciousness through prayer, reflection, meditation, conscious-altering substances, breathing techniques, yoga, fasting, and even just the power of undiluted observation.

You are invited to discover for yourself if you can step out of the ruts and habituated pathways formed by some of your beliefs and make the rest of your life the best, most precious and valuable time of your life.

New Challenges in the Game of Life

Our world is moving at such an enormous speed and with what sometimes appears to be an innocent but reckless disregard for the consequences of our decisions. Although it does not always recognize or willingly acknowledge it, our world needs the experience and wisdom elders and elders-in-training can offer.

This wisdom drawn from our victories and missteps, when

combined with the innocence, energy, and talent of youth, can bring enormous strength and nurturing to our world today. To paraphrase author Marianne Williamson, *The light at the center of things is who we are. And our mission in life is to uncover this light.*

So we invite you to move outside the ruts of ordinary perception, or if this is already a part of your practice, turn up the heat. How? Identify and experiment with the beliefs you hold.

Napoleon Hill, author of *Think and Grow Rich*, said, *"Whatever the mind can conceive and believe, it can achieve."* Valuable guidance! Henry Ford said it differently: *"Whether you think you can, or you think you can't—you're right."* And Marcel Proust, the great French writer, said, *"The real voyage of discovery consists not in seeking new landscapes, but in having new eyes."* In short, the beliefs we hold are the primary determiners of the scope, rhythm, quality, and boundaries of our lives.

A Primary and Limiting Belief

The belief that there is something wrong with getting old is one that can determine the amount of freedom or limitation we experience as we age.

Strange, isn't it? When we are young, most of us can't wait to be older. That is, until the next stage is called "getting old." Suddenly, we don't like this transition very much. In fact, most of us deal with this unavoidable reality by trying to deny it. And yet getting older is not only inevitable, but also natural; not only natural, but also—and here's the kicker—valuable!

It is like the third act of a play, the final chapters in a book, or the concluding movement of a symphony or ballet. Without getting old, there is no summation, no conclusion, no way to gain perspective on all of the earlier experiences that have unfolded in our previous acts, chapters, and movements. Nor can there be preparation for our graduation to the next higher level of consciousness or for the adding of our unique, distinct notes to life's song.

Please repeat this sentence a few times: *Getting older is not something to be denied and avoided; it is something to be accepted, experienced, honored, and celebrated.*

Life Rule

"Nothing splendid has ever been achieved except by those who dared believe that something inside them was superior to circumstance."

—BRUCE BARTON

Life Achievement

James Earl Jones continues to astound theater and film audiences into his eighties.

Life Tool

As you go through your day today, pause occasionally and ask yourself a few simple questions: "What beliefs about aging am I holding that prevent me from moving beyond the ruts of ordinary perception?" "Do these beliefs advance or retard my ability to experience more passion, engagement, and joy in this moment?"

It's Never Too Late
(or Too Soon)

"It doesn't interest me what you do for a living. I want to know what you ache for, and if you dare to dream of meeting your heart's longing. It doesn't interest me how old you are. I want to know if you will risk looking like a fool for love, for your dream, for the adventure of being alive."

—ORIAH MOUNTAIN DREAMER

One Day...

Do you remember believing one day you would be a great writer, painter, or composer? Do you remember wanting to invent a remarkable new product or social system, find the cure to a debilitating illness, be the one who rallies the troops to save the day, who enters the courtroom to right an injustice, or who throws your hat into the political ring to make a difference? Do you remember wanting to bring a brood of children into the world and raise them with genuine love and consciousness, to play the music or to sing the songs that echo in your heart? Do you remember wanting to be a coach, a teacher, a dancer, an actor, a choreographer, a cook, a carpenter, a fisherman, an astronaut, a mountain climber, a religious or spiritual leader, a humanitarian, or a healer?

Perhaps in your case, you did not know exactly what you wanted to do with your life but felt a longing you could not name, a restless tug to do something different from what others around you were doing. Perhaps that is still true for you. Please take a few moments to examine the beliefs you may be holding, answer some questions, and explore a few recommendations that can make the next stage of your journey not only more satisfying and rewarding, but also more in tune with the dream you came here to manifest.

If you take a little time to listen to your own inner wisdom, you will discover that this longing is still present and that by listening you will rediscover a pathway that can—no matter how old or young you are—lead you to live the dream you were born to live.

The Power of Your Dream

When you are in touch with your personal dream and stay true to its call, you are more creative, impassioned, and energetic, more connected to others, and more concerned about the well-being of the world. Your personal dream is the key to living more consciously and aging wisely and to fulfilling your spiritual promise.

Please do not just read the last paragraph and move on. Take a few deep breaths, go to that place in your heart where your dream still resides, and give yourself this gift of getting back in touch with your dream. Even if your first efforts only result in a vague sense of direction, a hint or a passing image, allow yourself this experience. Reconnect with that sense of hope, purpose, and passion. And if you feel the impulse to blow the dust off those paintbrushes; open the cover of the piano or your toolbox; or dig out that notebook full of ideas for that humanitarian project, business venture, novel, or something else you once were prompted to create, then do it! You will be very grateful.

Life Rule

"Dreams come true; without that possibility, nature would not incite us to have them."
—JOHN UPDIKE

Life Achievement

Carl Sandburg, one of America's great poets, wrote some of his most inspired poetry in his eighties.

Life Tool

Consider that each moment, each encounter, each thought, each word, and each action could be your last. If this is true, here are some questions you might find valuable:

Is this truly my best and highest use of this moment?
Am I improving my life and the lives of others, or am I just going through the motions?
Am I contributing my unique gifts to the world around me, or am I following a script written for me by someone else?

Who Are You and What Are You Doing Here?

"The real challenge of old age is to risk all habitual frames of reference and to open the mind to another field of possibility that lies beyond the physical. Having gained a foothold in the inner world, we then can encounter [life and] death with calm anticipation rather than horrifying fear."

—JOSEPH CHILTON PEARCE

Essential Questions

There is a contemporary British philosopher who has a rather provocative message on his voice mail. At first it seems quite ordinary. "Who are you, and what do you want?" the voice mail asks. The message, however, does not end there. It goes on to say, "If you think these questions are simple, think again! Most people come to this planet, live out a certain number of years, and never answer either of them."

So let us take our lead from this British philosopher and explore these two questions and also a third—*What are you doing here?* Our answers to these three questions will serve us very well on our journey.

In fact, if more of us answer these questions and follow George Burns's good advice—*it is better to be a failure at something you love than to be a success at something you hate*—more of us will live the lives we were born to live.

What Do You Believe?

Please take time to explore these three questions and some of the beliefs that may underlie them. Why? Because there is an ancient law of manifestation that states: *energy follows thought and manifestation follows energy.*

If you are willing to allow for the possibility that this law might be true, then you'll discover that your life experience is largely shaped by your thoughts and intentions and the actions that issue from them.

Do you see why the questions the British philosopher asks are so important? And why poet Mary Oliver asks, *"What do you plan to do with your one wild and precious life?"*

When each of us wrestles with these questions, everything will change. It will no longer be acceptable for anyone to pollute our planet; eliminate vital and essential species; violate the rights of others; or slaughter fellow human beings in the name of a religious, economic, or political philosophy. We will no longer allow our brethren to die of starvation while others live in excess—to let some live in despair while others frivolously pursue meaningless activities and ego-flattering goals. We will no longer accept systems that deny basic health care, medicines, and education to some while others overmedicate and overprescribe, or to accept limited and outmoded definitions of what it means to be a success and a true elder in our world.

So what do you believe?

Life Rule

"Success is the child of audacity."
—BENJAMIN DISRAELI

Life Achievement

Geronimo, the storied Native American warrior and chief, completed his autobiography at age seventy-seven.

Life Tool

Spend the next few days asking and seeking to answer this question—*What am I doing with this precious gift that is my life?* You do not have to change anything. Just let these questions live inside you and guide you and illuminate your thoughts, words, and deeds. In this space of openness, you may be surprised by what comes up and the impact it will have in the time ahead.

PART THREE

*Harvesting
the Wisdom
of Your Past*

"One would not think of throwing out the juice from a freshly squeezed orange and saving only the skin. So we might not want to focus exclusively on the images and memories from the past and discard the wisdom they contain."

—GEORGE CAPPANNELLI

Dealing with Incompletes

"Security is mostly a superstition. It does not exist in nature, nor do the children of men as a whole experience it. Avoiding danger is no safer in the long run than outright exposure. Life is either a daring adventure, or nothing."

—HELEN KELLER

If Only

Author Stephen Levine asks a fundamental question at the beginning of *A Year to Live*: *"What would you do if you only had one year to live?"*

A powerful question! In fact, a life-altering question—especially if you stop, even if only for a few moments, and let it lead you to that place where your truth resides. That is precisely what you can do in this chapter—explore this and other life-altering, life-enhancing, life-affirming questions.

Unlike the scenario that Stephen Levine's question suggests—imposing an artificial limit of one year to live—those of us in the second half of life may live another ten, twenty, or even fifty years or more. If this is true, why set aside hours from this active period and spend them sifting through somewhat challenging and difficult subjects? Isn't this the work we are supposed to do at the end of our lives?

We can, of course, put off working on living more consciously and aging wisely until some other time—if we are sure there will be enough "gas" of will and clarity left in our tank when that time arrives. We can also wait and do this work later if we don't mind spending the time between today and that future moment repeating some of the same mistakes and living a habitual life that may be less expansive, expressive, energetic, passionate, healthy, and grace-filled than it can be.

There are other benefits from doing this work now: greater

appreciation and gratitude, more energy and vitality, more passion, freedom, love, joy, contentment, and peace. Not a bad list, is it?

Of course, like all worthwhile things, these benefits require an investment on our part. Even though there are a number of infomercials and self-help programs that claim we can make money with no risk, lose weight with no exercise, or change our lives with no effort, there are no free rides.

Clearing the Decks

To experience these benefits, identify the incompletes you may be holding on to that are getting in your way of experiencing a more satisfying life. Each of us has a certain amount of our attention tied up in our incompletes. And this invested energy distracts us, drains our enthusiasm, and lowers our self-esteem.

If you are like most of us, each time you pass that closet, garage, gym, or classroom, every time you go into that stuffed drawer or storage space or find your body not as limber or light as you'd like it to be—in short, when you bump up against an incomplete—you probably renew that promise to learn, fix, clean, or begin doing something about it.

So why wait? Today's the perfect day to take a step toward living a more joyful life. And all you have to do is identify that closet, garage, promise, limited skill, or awkward relationship and create a more effective strategy for packing, cleaning, learning, and healing it.

The Incomplete Exercise

Start making a list of some of your incompletes. As you do, remember that no one is asking you to tackle them all. You are just making a list. Let your pen move easily without censorship.

Projects at home you have started and have not yet completed.
Projects at home you want to start.
Projects at work you have started and have not yet completed.
Projects at work you want to start.
Promises you made to yourself to learn some new skills that you have not yet fulfilled.
Relationships with parents, siblings, friends, and partners you want to improve.

This may not be an easy exercise, but please keep in mind how good you are going to feel when you have sifted through and reduced some of this baggage and clutter from your life.

Life Rule

"If I am not for myself, who will be? And when I am for myself, what am 'I'? And if not now, when?"
—HILLEL THE ELDER

Life Achievement

Peter Drucker, author and management guru, wrote *The Changing World of the Executive* at seventy-three.

Life Tool

Go back over your list and identify things that are no longer relevant or that you no longer have the desire or need to complete. Simply cross these off. As for things that remain on the list, especially those that have a particular emotional charge, the best way to deal with them is to pick a next physical action—open that desk drawer, pick up boxes for the garage, buy that missing screw or the paint, make a quick outline for that article, etc. Even this first step will give you a sense of how terrific you will feel when you free up the energy you currently have tied up in these incompletes.

Squeezing the Juice from the Fruit

"Enlightenment consists not merely in the seeing of luminous shapes and visions, but in making the darkness visible."

—CARL JUNG

Dealing Constructively with Your Past

In *From Age-ing to Sage-ing*, the book that helped launch the conscious aging movement in the United States, Zalman Schachter-Shalomi and Ronald S. Miller explore an essential step we can take to turn the grist of our past into the gold of the present and future. They call this step "harvesting."

As the name implies, harvesting is the process of reaping the fruits and the consequences from seeds we have sown or failed to sow earlier in our lives. It is a life review in which we take time to identify and turn the grist of our strengths and frailties, challenges and opportunities, our defeats, victories, and achievements, our incompletes as well as our contributions into the gold of processed experience and wisdom.

Harvesting is a form of cleansing, and, if we allow it to be, a valuable healing and life repair. It gives us a chance to make sense of our past; heal old wounds; let go of old baggage; and regain our emotional, physical, mental, and spiritual balance so the lives we lead today and tomorrow will be richer, more rewarding, and more fulfilling.

Schachter-Shalomi and Miller suggest other benefits:

We also appreciate the friendships we have nurtured, the young people we have mentored, and our wider involvements on behalf of the community, the nation, and ultimately the Earth. Harvesting can be experienced from within as quiet self-appreciation or from without through the honor, respect, and recognition received from family members, relatives, colleagues at work, and mentees.

Harvesting Steps

1. Identify and explore the major events of your life from an emotional and psychological standpoint.
2. Clear away some of the clutter and excess baggage (incompletes) and make sense of your experience.
3. Answer important spiritual and philosophic questions: What does life mean to you? Why are you here? What does death mean? Is there a Next, or is this all there is?
4. Get your personal affairs in order—wills, powers of attorney, medical directives, funeral arrangements, etc.

You have already begun the harvesting process in the work you have done on reclaiming your dreams and on eliminating your incompletes. In fact, you have done some of the heavy lifting. Now, you can continue this process of turning more of the straw of your experience into the gold of learning and higher consciousness. This will involve identifying both the good stuff—achievements, accomplishments, and lessons learned—as well as what you may believe is the less attractive stuff.

What you may find is that when viewed from the short-term perspective, the end of a friendship, the loss of a job or career opportunity, a financial hardship, an accident, an illness, or a divorce may have seemed negative. However, when reviewed from the longer-term "harvesting" perspective, you may discover that the job you lost or that opportunity you believe you missed actually opened the way for a new career direction or proved to be the impetus to start a new business. That accident or financial setback may have led you to a shift in values or priorities. The end of a relationship or the loss of a loved one may have opened the door to greater strength within yourself and perhaps even to a new love.

So please remember Marcel Proust's quote: "*The voyage of discovery consists not in seeking new landscapes, but in having new eyes.*" It will help you engage in this life review with the curiosity and neutral observation of a reporter attempting to uncover the truth, and with the enthusiasm of one who is about to make new discoveries.

You may also consider this clue from Stephen Levine:

We look back at our life, not as if we still owned it but as though we were about to give it up. A recollection of the past as though this might be the last sip of that old wine, the last kiss from that departed lover, the last time to appreciate a life so full of our very human experience.

Life Rule

"If you only expect the best, you very often get it."

—W. SOMERSET MAUGHAM

Life Achievement

Martha Graham, who some regard as the grand dame of American dance, was still choreographing new work well into her nineties.

Life Tool

Identify several of your most outstanding life achievements as well as some of the experiences you considered failures or particularly difficult moments. First, take time to feel the feelings associated with your achievements. Savor them and anchor them inside you. In the years ahead, these strong, positive feelings will provide you with energy and motivation you may need to deal with adversity or regain your sense of balance. Regarding those you consider failures or difficult moments, as you review them, pay special attention to what you learned and how they sometimes paved the way for your later achievements.

The Best Is Yet to Be

Whose Beliefs Are You Living?

"If we looked back on our lives with complete honesty, many of us would conclude, 'I was lived by my parents; I was lived by my teachers; I was lived by society.'"

—ZALMAN SCHACHTER-SHALOMI

Believing vs. Knowing

Ever stopped to consider where your beliefs come from? As a next step in your process of living the life you were born to live, you are invited to do this now. It's not hard. Just identify some of your beliefs about aging, about the options and possibilities this time of life holds for you, about your fears and worries, your victories and celebrations, and even some of your confusions and regrets. In short, explore the primary beliefs you hold that have shaped your life to date and will, if left unexamined and unchanged, most certainly shape and perhaps limit your life in the years ahead.

Carl Jung, one of the fathers of psychology, took great pains to point out that believing is very different than knowing. Beliefs rest mainly on the opinions held by others and, in many cases, a majority of others who make up our world—people in our families, churches, schools, businesses, ethnic and religious group, nations, etc. This does not, however, make them correct.

Alan Watts, author and spiritual teacher, had this to say on the subject: *"Belief…is the insistence that the truth is what one would 'lief' or (will or) wish to be."*

Knowing, by comparison, is based on one's personal experience. Sometimes our experience is the result of faulty assumptions or incorrect information, but in the end, experience is a great teacher and the knowing we arrive at aligns with an inner yardstick each of us possesses— a yardstick that is far more accurate than someone else's beliefs.

Knowing sometimes comes to us from an intuitive flash or insight often not immediately verifiable to others or directly linked to something that has happened in our present lifetime. But it still has certainty and undeniability. Knowing sometimes manifests through a flight of fancy or imagination. For example, as a boy, Albert Einstein dreamed of riding a beam of light through space. Later, when his skill in mathematics allowed him to do so, he followed this dream and formulated the Theory of Relativity.

Although knowing is much more powerful than believing, in this age when science, technology, and aggregated opinions are used as the primary measurement of what is real and what is not, beliefs shape much of our experience. Of course, this is not a new path for humanity—history is full of examples. At one point in history, the prevailing belief was that the world was flat. When one considers the impact of media in the Information Age and how it often trumpets the same information over and over—as if repetition was a path to truth—it is not hard to understand how beliefs unfortunately often win out over knowing. This is especially unfortunate because our world would be richer, truer, more balanced and aligned with nature if each of us only used our beliefs as temporary crutches on the road to our knowing.

Another reason to pay close attention to where our beliefs come from is the law of manifestation mentioned earlier—*energy follows thought and manifestation follows energy.* If thought equals knowing, what we manifest is powerful and aligned. If, however, thought equals believing, what we manifest is a lot less stable and requires interpretation and translation by others. And whenever we have to depend on translators and interpreters, we run the risk of being manipulated, even if unintentionally.

Tracing the Source

Since Dr. Jung and a number of other wise individuals have invited us to remember that believing is not nearly as valuable or powerful as knowing, it would seem that a next and valuable step would be to identify where our beliefs come from.

Here's a starter list of categories of beliefs. All you have to do is identify at least one primary belief you hold in each of these categories and decide whether it rests on the opinions of others or your own knowing.

Beliefs I Hold About

Youth
Success
Health
Money
Meaning and Purpose
Aging
Death
What Happens After Death
God, Spirit, Oneness…

Life Rule

"O God, help me to believe the truth about myself, no matter how beautiful it is!"
—MACRINA WIEDERKEHR

Life Achievement

Toni Morrison, author and activist, received the Nobel Prize for Literature at sixty-two.

Life Tool

Now that you are beginning to remember how much more valuable knowing is than believing, you may want to experiment with how powerful, joyful, inviting, and successful your life can be when you base your thoughts, words, and actions on your own knowing. Look over your list of primary beliefs and put an "M" beside those based on your knowing and an "O" beside those based on the beliefs of others. Then ask yourself, "What will my life be like when I learn to think, speak, and act based on my knowing?"

Limiting Beliefs, Limited Life

"No longer needing to compete and to be acceptable, likable, and all those other things considered respectable in society, people are finally uncaged in their elder years, free to release energies and capacities that the culture restrained in them when they were younger."

—JEAN HOUSTON

The Limiting Power of Limiting Beliefs

There is a particular category of beliefs—limiting beliefs—that negatively impact the shape of our lives.

Consider this: 1,200 words a minute, 50,000 separate thoughts a day. That's the estimated speed at which we think and the average number of discrete thoughts we have each day. Clearly this adds up to a whole lot of thinking and a lot of beliefs that impact our lives—especially if they are limiting beliefs. What is a limiting or negative belief? Something that causes us to restrict, prevent, obstruct, and resist the natural flow of our lives.

In the language of computers there is a phrase—garbage in, garbage out—meaning that the quality of the output we can expect from our computers depends primarily on the quality of the data we input. Since computers are, in some ways, modeled after the functioning of the human brain, it certainly follows that the same rules about quality of content also apply to the information (accurate or inaccurate) we store there.

Limiting beliefs—especially those that have been passed on to us by someone who in turn unconsciously accepted them from others—are like pirated software. They do not arrive in a package from "the manufacturer" free of viruses. Instead, negative beliefs are unauthenticated opinions, which, over time and through repetition, are mistaken for truth. For example, people once believed that beyond the borders of the known was the realm of dragons.

Clearly, if ancient explorers had not sailed right through this and other limiting beliefs, much of the modern world would have never been discovered. Indeed, in many ways, history is a record of false boundaries and limited capacities that have been exploded by those courageous enough to go beyond them.

The Amazing Power of Positive Beliefs

Fortunately, not all of the beliefs we hold are negative. For example, if we believe that we can accomplish something, that we are competent, worthy, decent, effective, productive, etc., then we have a very real shot at eventually demonstrating that competence, effectiveness, etc., and consequently living more satisfying and successful lives.

Remember those quotes by Henry Ford and Napoleon Hill, *"Whether you think you can, or you think you can't—you're right"* and *"Whatever the mind can conceive and believe, it can achieve."*

Dr. David Hawkins, another courageous adventurer, has spent decades studying the phenomenon of energy and its impact on the physical universe and physical manifestation. In his book *Power vs. Force*, he explores how applied kinesiology (muscle testing) can help identify a corresponding frequency associated with each emotional state (and the positive or negative beliefs associated with it). The more positive the emotional state, the higher and more powerful the frequency and the more powerful the resulting physical manifestation. According to Dr. Hawkins:

One individual [who calibrates] at 300 [the level of willingness] counterbalances 90,000 individuals [who calibrate] below level 200. One individual at level 400 [reason] counterbalances 400,000 individuals below level 200. One individual at level 600 [peace] counterbalances 10 million individuals below level 200.

Amazing to consider, isn't it?

Life Rule

"What makes greatness is starting something that lives after you."

—RALPH W. SOCKMAN

Life Achievement

Lionel Hampton, American jazz great, was still performing into his nineties.

Life Tool

Identifying limited beliefs and replacing them with positive ones may be one of the most important things you can do. Remember that energy follows thought and manifestation follows energy, so what you think and how you think shapes your world.

The Gift That Keeps on Giving

"Forgiveness does not change the past,
but it does enlarge the future."

—PAUL BOESE

More Than Just Another Step

Most of us have, of course, practiced various forms of forgiveness in our lives. In fact, the concept is so familiar that some of us tend to take it for granted and, as a result, practice it rather superficially. There is, however, an ancient Hawaiian practice called ho'oponopono that can help us experience more of the real grace and power of forgiveness.

Dr. Ihaleakala Hew Len was a health practitioner associated with one of the most difficult wards in a psychiatric facility in Hawaii. This ward was reserved for those who were unlikely to be released—ever. During his tenure there, however, Dr. Hew Len demonstrated an unusually high success rate that assisted many of these psychiatric inmates to not only improve, but also be rehabilitated and released.

His approach mirrored the Buddhist concept of the unity of all life and the deep interrelationship between all human beings. Dr. Hew Len did not treat the dysfunctions present in his patients as separate from himself, but rather as tendencies present within his own nature. Taking responsibility for these tendencies, he turned within and asked for forgiveness for them from his Higher Power. When he felt this forgiveness well up from deep inside him—not only for himself, but also for his patients—he expressed deep gratitude and love to the Source. Over time, this approach bore the remarkable level of healing discussed above.

Beyond Guilt and Resentment

Experimenting with this version of ho'oponopono will allow you to open your heart when it closes and to put down long-held burdens of anger, fear, disappointment, and particularly feelings of guilt (over things you have done) and resentment (over things others have done to you). It can help you heal past and current relationships and to live more fully and freely in the present moment where all things are possible. This is why it is called "the gift that keeps on giving."

To benefit from this experience, you might want to temporarily suspend your belief that forgiving others lets them off the hook for the harm they may have caused you or that forgiving yourself for your insensitive, unkind, and harmful acts lets you off the hook.

No matter which of these beliefs you may hold, the truth is, as Lewis B. Smedes once said, *"to forgive is to set a prisoner free and to discover that the prisoner was you."*

Bishop Desmond Tutu, who, along with Nelson Mandela, helped establish the restorative justice movement in South Africa, said, *"Without forgiveness, there is no future."* Indeed, without our willingness to truly forgive ourselves and others for real or perceived sins and transgressions, we remain prisoners of the past.

Four Simple Steps
on the Road to Freedom

You are invited to experiment with one of Dr. Hew Len's ho'oponopono forgiveness processes. This practice may appear simple, and indeed it is, but that does not mean it is not powerful and restorative. So find a quiet place where you will not be interrupted for just a little while, take a few deep, slow breaths, and then read these simple phrases over a few times until you are familiar with them:

I'm sorry.
Please forgive me.
Thank you.
I love you.

When you are ready, close your eyes and call to mind the image of someone you believe may have caused you some harm or discomfort. You may want to begin with the image of someone you believe has caused you relatively minor harm—like a disagreement you had with your significant other earlier in the day or a small amount of impatience or criticism a friend exhibited toward you.

Hold his or her image in your mind and keep repeating the four statements until you feel your heart open to this person. Once this occurs, express your gratitude and then call to mind the image of someone else who you believe you may have harmed. Again, repeat these four statements until you feel your guilt begin to lessen or dissolve.

Lewis B. Smedes gives us another very important clue:

"You will know that forgiveness has begun when you recall those who hurt you [or you have hurt] and feel the power to wish them well."

Make a two-part list—people who have hurt or offended you, and people you have hurt or offended. Each day, pick one person from both sides of your list and hold that person's or your own image in your mind and use Dr. Len's ho'oponopono statements or whatever forgiveness method you might prefer. Do this each day for thirty days, and notice how much lighter and freer you feel.

Life Rule

"Forgive or relive."
—ANONYMOUS

Life Achievement

Country music legend Willie Nelson tours and creates new albums with his distinctive voice in his eighties.

Life Tool

Your road to conscious living and wise aging passes directly through the territory of forgiveness. So you are invited to participate in a thirty-day forgiveness process.

PART FOUR

Here and Now—the Road to Living the Life You Were Born to Live

"I wasted a lot of my life attempting to be like everyone else. Elderhood gives me permission to delight in my uniqueness. I've discovered that as we age, we don't become more like others; we become more like ourselves."

—PAM, HOSPICE COUNSELOR,
EXCERPT FROM *FROM AGE-ING TO SAGE-ING*

Living & Learning
in the Now

"Keep the gold and keep the silver,
but give us wisdom."

—ARABIAN PROVERB

Present Moment Awareness

In *The Power of Now* and *A New Earth*, author and spiritual teacher Eckhart Tolle explores the value of living in the now. Ram Dass in *Be Here Now* and *Still Here* illuminates these practices as essential as well. You may want to give yourself the gift of reading them.

Let's follow their lead and learn to place our attention in this one unique, distinct instant—this point of power, this choice point that has never occurred for us in quite the same way before and never will again.

As you read these words, expand your focus to also include the flow of your breath, the beating of your heart, sounds happening around you, smells, the temperature of the air, and quality of the light. Notice that although your mind may appear to be occupied with these words and their meaning, your senses are constantly tuning in to all that is going on around and within you. The universe is constantly giving us opportunities to learn, and sometimes even a small expansion of focus to include heart as well as head allows the magic happening between, around, and within the words to become apparent.

Jack Kornfield, mindfulness and meditation teacher, says, *"The power of loving-kindness, the power of those living from the heart, makes the power of armies and technology seem like child's play. For it is the heart force that brings all life, that creates all life, that moves through us."*

This same phenomenon is described by a Zen Master who is reputed to have said, *"The greedy one gathered all the cherries, while the simple one tasted all the cherries in one."*

The present moment is the only moment we have and the only moment in which anything actually happens. Remember, our failure to be aware of what is happening within and around us in each moment limits the richness of our lives. In fact, one can liken times when we fall victim to the past or become preoccupied with the future to taking only a few hurried bites at a huge feast. While it may temporarily satiate some of our hunger, in the end, we miss what truly nourishes us.

Other Keys to Living in the Now

Explore living in the now—not just intellectually, but viscerally. And when you forget—a thing all of us do regularly—acknowledge it and return your attention to the present moment by following your breath and focusing on what you are seeing, hearing, tasting, smelling, and feeling. Just now! Just here! Just you!

Gratitude is another key. Gratitude for whatever is happening within and around you in this moment—even if your mind wants to label it as unpleasant, boring, confusing, or even painful. Honor what is going on and you will discover new opportunities and experiences and new levels of interaction with yourself and with others.

Learning in the Now

Another valuable gift you can give yourself is the understanding that everything you truly want or need to learn is right in front of you in this present moment.

Health issues? This is where your learning can be found. Relationship challenges with your spouse or partner, one of your children, or a friend? This is your next lesson. Obstacles at work, staff or client disharmony, challenges in the organization you volunteer for, or the club you support—your next best lesson. Internal confusion about what to do with your energy and talent? You guessed it!

You do not have to enroll in a graduate program, sign up for classes at your local community college, or take out a student loan to discover this next lesson. Simply look at the syllabus called your daily life, and you will find more than enough pertinent lessons. Then, if you choose to take that graduate program or community college class, or engage a therapist or coach to assist you, the benefit will be enormous. For you will understand what you want to learn.

On the subject of when to start learning your next lesson, that answer is also simple. Now! And the good news is that you do not need to apply and wait for admission to begin. All you have to do is realize that the earth is a live-as-you-go, study-where-you-are, moment-by-moment school. Your best learning will be found at the checkout counter of your local market; in your next conversation with one of your children, your spouse, or a friend; in your next personal interaction, email, phone call, or meeting; on an airplane; while stuck in traffic; or the next time you are out in nature.

Each thought, word, and action in each moment holds your next lesson; each person you meet is your next teacher. The present moment is your next and best opportunity to live the life you were born to live.

Life Rule

"We can do noble acts without ruling the earth and sea."
—ARISTOTLE

Life Achievement

Frank Lloyd Wright, one of America's preeminent architects, designed some of his most imaginative and celebrated buildings in his eighties.

Life Tool

Pay attention to what is happening in this moment. Whether with others, by yourself, at work, or at home, what is happening now is your doorway to your next discovery. This moment is not a place to pass through on the way to someplace or something else. It is the end and the beginning. It is your moment to claim your power and to be your authentic and original self.

The Extraordinary
Gift of Being
Curious

"Nobody grows old by merely living a number of years. We grow old by deserting our ideals."

—SAMUEL ULLMAN

The Miracle of Life

Dorothy Parker said, *"The cure for boredom is curiosity. There is no cure for curiosity."* So, if you want to live more mindfully and joyfully, stop pretending you know it all or have done it all and start being open to what you do not yet know and have not yet done. In this way, life will again become a real-time adventure and each "now" another opportunity for richness and wonder.

In order to discover more effective solutions to old problems and new alternatives to habitual patterns, stop pretending you have it all together and start being curious about life again. Curiosity is a key to living in the *now*, and now is the only time and place we can experience the magical, the marvelous, and the unknown.

Ralph Waldo Emerson once said, *"What lies behind us and what lies before us are tiny matters compared to what lies within us."* If you doubt the value of this recommendation, spend a little time observing children. Notice how curious they are, how involved they are in their moment-to-moment experiences. Pay attention to how open they are to life—learning, experimenting, making things up, acting things out, and making new friends, sometimes immediately. See how unafraid they are to be silly.

Unfortunately, as we grow older, we too often assume that school is over and that we already know or are supposed to know things. We get smug and certain or habitual and defensive and, as a result, our world gets smaller or duller.

Kind of ridiculous, don't you think, to go through the second half of life clinging tenaciously to what we think we know and, as a result, miss opportunities to be all of the things we can be in the years ahead?

So have fun seeing the world with new, more compassionate, connected, and receptive eyes. Set aside those old beliefs and start exploring the landscape of your life as if you were young, innocent, and courageous again. Remember—*"lest you be as children you will not enter the kingdom of heaven."*

Steps to Being Curious

Experiment

Change the way you look, the route you drive to your home or office, what you do for entertainment, books you read, and food you eat. Literally change your interactions with the physical world, and you will change your experience of life.

Change your perspective

See life from someone else's point of view. Imagine what the things you do every day look, sound, and feel like to others—younger people, peers who are more or less fortunate than you, people who don't speak your language, and those who are older than you.

Change your physical environment and habits

Change the color of a room and arrangement of the furniture. Travel to new places. Take up a new hobby or sport, something you've never been good at, and experience the fun of not knowing.

Be curious about the way things work

Take courses. Take things apart and learn how to put them together. Watch, observe, understand! And not just with physical objects. What happens between the notes in a musical composition, in the space between breaths, in the instant between laughter and tears, between this moment and the next one?

Life Rule

"Each of us needs to withdraw from the cares which will not withdraw from us."
—MAYA ANGELOU

Life Achievement

Romana Kryzanowska taught Pilates after learning it from Joseph Pilates more than seventy years ago. Romana was ninety when she passed away in 2013.

Life Tool

Experiment with creating a daily intention. This practice can help you keep your focus during the day and provide you with a touchstone that you can return to at the end of the day. Your daily intention might be just to "be present." Setting clear intentions may be one of the most important things you do today. And don't forget, at the end of today, reflect back on the day and ask yourself, "How true was I to my intention and what did I learn?"

Mastering the Three Great Illusions

"The beginning of wisdom is
a firm grip on the obvious."

—ANONYMOUS

Valuable Secrets to Present Moment Awareness

Three illusions significantly limit our lives and prevent us from living the life we were born to live. These are *control, safety,* and *security.* Learning to master them can be your next and most important step on this journey.

Control

In this world where science and technology are revered, many of us live under the illusion that we can control things—our physical environment, our financial future, our careers, and in some instances, even the people around us. Yet, if we look closely at the most important events in our lives, most of us will admit that for all intents and purposes, life has been pretty much outside of our control from the start. We did not control our birth, and the majority of us will not control our death.

Even the basic physical functions that allow us to stay alive—respiration, digestion, elimination, and circulation—are autonomic. And some have suggested this is a very fortunate thing.

If you look closely and without ego at your life, you will also admit that many of the really meaningful and consequential events you've experienced fall into the category of surprises, unexpected events, and what Carl Jung called synchronicity—"chance exceeding probability." Here are some examples: the moment the love of your life showed up; the day your career took one of its most surprising and beneficial turns (a turn which might have seemed negative at first); changes in your health that prompted you to adopt new practices and sometimes even a new way of life; chance encounters with people you did not like at first and who later became your close friends; unanticipated intersections with allies and mentors; and sudden flashes of insight and inspiration that brought you wonderful gifts.

Control is pretty much a fabrication, a kind of hoping against hope on the part of a species that likes to think it is "master of the universe" but for whom this complex thing called life still remains pretty much beyond comprehension.

Safety and Security

What about safety and security? Many of us spend as much, if not more, of our lives in search of safety and security as we do trying to exercise control. In fact, if we are honest, we will admit that we cling to this holy triumvirate of control, safety, and security with a tenacity that ranges from the compulsive to the obsessive.

On the surface, of course, some of us appear to succeed in our relationship with safety and security. We accumulate a certain amount of wealth and use it to erect buffers between us and the world: gated communities, 401(k) plans and other investment accounts, special insurance policies, extra health coverage plans, investment properties, and in some cases, even private security personnel. With all those buffers in place, we appear, at least on the surface, to be pretty safe and secure.

If you look a little closer at these conditions, however, you will also discover that just like control, safety and security are illusions. For no matter how much money we have, how many private clubs we belong to, or whether protective gates surround our communities, no matter how many special health plans or insurance policies we own, in the end, none of them truly protect us from aging, illness, loss of loved ones, intersections with unhappiness, loss of meaning and purpose, and ultimately our own deaths, and none of them ensure that we will be more loving, generous, and conscious.

Surrender Is the Key

Instead, surrender, acceptance, and trust are the real keys to a successful life. This does not mean throwing in the towel and rolling over on life or not paying attention to the upkeep of our homes, payment of bills, making and monitoring investments, taking care of our health, nurturing our relationships, or ordering our affairs. Surrender, acceptance, and trust are not synonymous with indifference, inattention, and disinterest.

As many wise beings before us have said, we do the best we can do, hold the highest thoughts possible, live life according to our truest set of values, and ultimately trust in the flow of life and in the higher order of things.

Indeed, a very wise old man, a master sculptor from Spain named José de Creeft, who was still carving and modeling remarkable pieces well into his nineties, said, *"It is not our job to worry about the music. It is our job to become the best instruments we can so that the music of God can play through us."*

Life Rule

"Everyone wants to be somebody; nobody wants to grow."

—JOHANN WOLFGANG VON GOETHE

Life Achievement

Pablo Casals, considered by many to be one of the world's greatest cellists, played his last concert in Israel at age ninety-six.

Life Tool

Take a few moments and reflect on some of the achievements and events of your life. Pay close attention to the part you played in the outcome, and then pay equal homage to the part fate, good fortune, grace, other people, remarkable synchronicities, and unexpected surprises played as well. Notice how these things seemingly outside your control contributed in ways that served you and that you would not have thought of or executed on your own.

PART FIVE

Charting a Remarkable Course for Your Future

"Throughout most of history, elders occupied honored roles in society as sages and seers, leaders and judges, guardians of the traditions, and instructors of the young. They were revered as gurus, shamans, wise old men and women who helped guide the social order and who initiated spiritual seekers into the mysteries of inner space."

—ZALMAN SCHACHTER-SHALOMI AND RONALD MILLER

Packing for
the Future

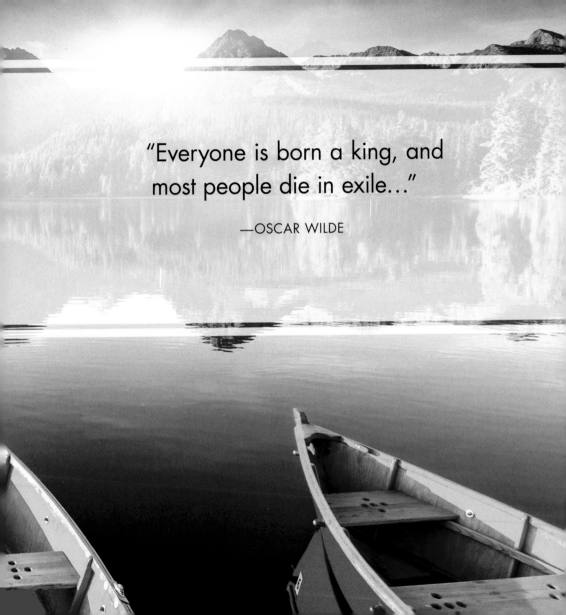

"Everyone is born a king, and most people die in exile..."

—OSCAR WILDE

Know Where You Are Going

Most of us know that the more information we have about our destination, the more likely we will pack the right gear, bring the right clothing, and, if traveling to an exotic or dangerous destination, get the required inoculations. In short, the more we know about our destination, the greater the likelihood we will have a successful trip.

Good travelers also make sure things are in order at home and at work before they depart. It is one of the ways they give themselves relative peace of mind while away and limit the quagmire of issues they encounter when they return.

Although some of us understand this and, as a result, make reasonably good holiday travelers, some of us do not do nearly as good of a job traveling through the stages of this journey called life. So in this section of the book, you're encouraged to look at some of the practical things you would be wise to pay greater attention to in order to make your journey more successful and enjoyable.

A Few More Words about Destination

Before talking about what you can do to prepare for your life journey, you may want to revisit the fundamental question about destination. Those two questions the British philosopher asks his callers, plus the third question posed, will assist you in charting a course for your future.

Who are you?
What do you want?
What are you doing here?

If you have not given much thought to them, you might want to do that now. If you have already done this, you might find it helpful to revisit your previous conclusions. After all, tastes and needs change over time, and a destination or goal you thought appropriate at forty, or even sixty, might not be right at eighty or beyond. To paraphrase T. S. Eliot's caution: *Fare forward, travelers; you who arrive at your terminus are not the same as you who departed.*

Once you have given some additional thought to your destination, turn your attention to some practical things you would be wise to have in place—financial and living wills, insurance and healthcare coverage, a family trust, and a little rainy-day fund.

Practical Considerations

Those of us who are in the second half of life would be wise to reexamine our priorities and values and evaluate how we use our time, the kind of environments we live in, and the type and amount of goods and services we require.

Physical

Take the best possible care of your body, for it is the instrument that allows you to experience life. Also pay attention to doing what is necessary to take care of your physical environment and your finances.

Emotional

Take steps to keep your emotional body in balance—harvesting, dealing with incompletes, practicing forgiveness, expressing a lot of gratitude, and sharing your love.

Mental

Exercise your mind with quality stimulation. Learn new languages, master new disciplines, explore new interests, reflect, exercise your creativity and imagination, and use supplements and foods that can increase your mental acuity.

Spiritual

Pray, meditate, spend time in nature, and spend time in silence.

Taken together, these practices will assist you in balancing your body, mind, emotions, and spirit and in keeping your physical environment and financial well-being in the best shape possible.

Also remember acceptance, surrender, and trust, and when the music of life brings you unexpected twists, challenges, and gifts, flow with them with as much grace and love as possible.

Life Rule

"There is no cure for birth or death save to enjoy the interval."
—GEORGE SANTAYANA

Life Achievement

James Lipton, host of *Inside the Actors Studio*, one of television's longest-running and most successful programs, is in his eighties.

Life Tool

Make a plan and check it twice. Be attentive to details, be thoughtful about your needs, and set aside sufficient time to identify the things you need to do and the specific steps you want to take to ensure that you are packing well for the second half of your life.

Dreams vs. Desires

"Only when we find the spring of wisdom in our own life can it flow to future generations."

—THICH NHAT HANH

Giving Your Best

Since our ability to chart a successful course for the future involves getting in touch with the dream we have come here to manifest, it seems important to differentiate between dreams and desires. It is also important to free up energy we currently have committed to our desires so we can use it to fulfill our dreams.

A desire is anything we have wanted to do, have, or be at any time during our lives to date. You know the litany—"I want this or that, to be with him or her. I want to go there, buy that, experience this, own that, become this, and so on." Hundreds, thousands, perhaps hundreds of thousands of desires have accumulated thus far in our lives, and each has some of our life energy and attention tied up in it.

Why concern ourselves with this? Remember that law of manifestation—*energy follows thought and manifestation follows energy.* If you've tested its validity, you now know that what you focus on is what you ultimately manifest. Focus on insignificant, transient, and relatively meaningless things, focus on worry, doubt, and your inability to do something—and that is what you manifest. Focus on remarkable, life-sustaining, uplifting things, and that will be your result.

Desires vs. Dreams

It should not surprise any of us in this restless, consumption-focused world that the distinction between desires and dreams has become as blurred as the difference between believing and knowing, looking and seeing, and hearing and listening. Indeed, for many of us, these terms have become synonymous, and yet the differences between them are enormous.

Desires (you can substitute the word *wants* or *hungers* as well) issue from a perception, belief, or feeling that there is absence or lack. Because desires are the offspring of emptiness, our efforts to satisfy them cannot be successful. Indeed, one cannot want and have at the same time, nor can one satisfy one's hunger by eating the menu instead of the meal.

Dreams, by comparison, are the legitimate issue of our souls seeking expression and manifestation in this journey called life. This does not refer to our night dreams, but instead to the flashes of inspiration and intuition, insights and knowing, that come to us as prompts and messages from our hearts. Dreams are the hints that, when we are brave enough to follow them, will lead us to discover new landscapes and destinations of remarkable individual and collective value.

By comparison to the loud trumpeting of desires, dreams can sometimes be quiet and so subtle we almost miss them. This subtlety often causes us to doubt their reality. And yet, we all have had moments when our muse has whispered in our ear, moments when hints and prompts come up at night when we can't sleep or in quiet moments during the day when we least expect them. Hints sometimes surface as daydreams. Sometimes they arise like mirages, there one instant, luminous and enticing, and gone and almost forgotten the next. And in a world where there are so many desires fighting for our attention and seducing us—not just once, but again and again—it's easy to brush these quieter prompts aside.

As you identify the course you want to chart going forward, you would be wise to stop going for the brass ring and the ever-elusive carrot of desire and focus instead on the authentic look and feel of your deeper dream. Your dream will open doorways to new ways of living and being and generate genuine joy, lasting satisfaction, and enduring love. Your dream will lead you to meaning and purpose, allowing you to harness your potential and fulfill your destiny.

Reflect on the following three questions:

What is one dream I still want to experience or manifest in this lifetime?

What kind of difference would expressing or manifesting this dream make in my life?

How would fulfilling this dream contribute to the lives of others?

Marianne Williamson said, *"It is our light, not our darkness, that most frightens us."* Some of us are afraid of standing out, of shining too brightly. As you explore your dreams, do not let the fear of the light be what prevents you from experiencing life.

Life Rule

"It is never too late to be what you might have been."

—GEORGE ELIOT

Life Achievement

Nelson Mandela became the first black president of South Africa at seventy-five.

Life Tool

Pay attention to the difference between your desires and your dreams. And if you want to live the life you were born to live, stop focusing on desires and start living your dreams.

Let Passion Lead

"It is not a matter of thinking a great deal, but of loving a great deal, so do whatever arouses you most to love."

—SAINT TERESA OF AVILA

A Key to an Extraordinary Future

Having talked about the difference between desires (wants/hungers) and dreams, let's explore one of the most important qualities we have at our disposal to help us live our dreams. Passion. Your passion will, if you allow it, lead you to manifest your dream. It is the grand differentiator, the great discerner, and the extraordinary enabler on your journey into the future.

Passion is not lust or greed—two experiences that are often mistaken for it. It is not a restlessness or hunger that entangles us in desires. These cheap and flimsy imitations do not lead us to fulfill our dreams.

Lust and greed, like the desires they prompt, are sirens that draw us toward the rocks of mediocrity and regret with their garish and seductive song. They cause us to miss that place of quiet surety within our hearts, that place of surrender and mindfulness. Instead, they promote willfulness, desperation, and aggression that lead us at times to abuse others and violate our own cherished values.

The Genuine Article

By comparison, passion, like knowing, is the genuine article. It is authentic, distinct, and original. It may not feel at first like something major or even make itself known in obvious ways. But like a spring that is only a trickle at its source, our passion will gather strength, power, and momentum. And if we follow it, it can lead us to an infinite ocean of meaning and purpose.

Passion sometimes begins as a whisper, at other times as a sudden, powerful, and undeniable force that breaks through the fabric of everyday reality and announces its presence. But no matter how it manifests in your life, your willingness to follow it will grant you a second half of life far different and more meaningful than the first half.

Even if you were blessed to find your career path early in life and it is the path you will walk for the rest of your life, the difference between letting your passion lead you and running after your desire to succeed is immense.

Let Passion Lead

What do you do if you know your passion does not reside in what you are currently doing? As hard as it may seem at first, either find a way to bring your passion into what you are doing or let passion lead you to your next opportunity.

Passion is an inside out job. If you get the inkling that you have mistaken passion for desire, be wise and shift your attention from your head to your heart. Do what you do—not by running after need, greed, fame, or attention—but instead, by giving your allegiance to your heart, to love, connection, and genuine service.

Life Rule

"Nothing great in the world has ever been accomplished without passion."
—GEORG WILHELM FRIEDRICH HEGEL

Life Achievement

Giuseppe Verdi composed his opera *Otello* at seventy-three and *Falstaff* when he was close to eighty.

Life Tool

Close your eyes for a moment or two and ask yourself: "What do I most care about, and what would I express in my life if I did not believe I was limited or motivated by money, concern about time, or some other obligation or responsibility?" Then open your eyes and start living your dream.

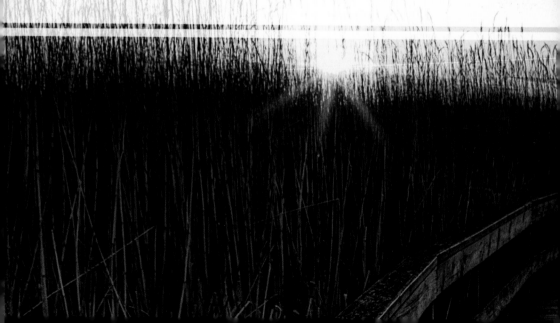

The Best Is Yet to Come

"When love and skill work together,
expect a masterpiece."

—JOHN RUSKIN

Another Gift That Keeps on Giving

As we prepare to complete this stage of our journey together, let's return briefly to the conversation about living and learning in the now, for our intention to live with a greater moment-by-moment awareness is an invaluable key to all the best that is yet to come.

You may find it strange that the idea that some of what lies ahead—including the real and challenging aspects of aging and dying—could be included in this "The Best Is Yet to Come" chapter. But if you have taken to heart some of the concepts and recommendations, participated in some of the exercises, and allowed the short inspirational stories about others to touch you, then you probably have already begun revisiting some of your values and reshaping some of your priorities in ways that will ensure that what lies ahead of you—all of it—will not only be acceptable, but also unique, engaging, appropriate, inspiring, and even quite remarkable.

The practice of being present in this and every other moment is one of the genuine gifts that will keep on giving to each of us and to everyone we touch every day for the rest of our lives. As will the understanding that we are never too old or too young to live our dreams. These things will assist us in engaging and benefiting more fully from each experience and every interaction. They will allow us to uncover the essence in each moment so that instead of living in a divided house—fluctuating between our heads and our hearts, between the past and the future—we can benefit from the wise advice of Thich Nhat Hanh, peace activist and teacher of present moment awareness: *On the in breath say, "I have arrived." On the out breath, "I am home."* No matter how lost in the past or future you get, these two simple phrases will bring you back into present moment awareness and to all of the gifts that await you.

There is a woman who seeks neither the spotlight nor acknowledgment but who embodies this awareness. When asked how she is doing, she responds with this simple phrase: *"I'm just right!"* No matter what is going on—something challenging or easy, awkward or elevating—she says, *"I'm just right!"*

Such a simple and yet profound statement. When we are present, and acknowledge and accept whatever is going on as our reality, we discover that "what is" is precisely what is supposed to be. So follow the flow instead of trying to push the river. *"I am here. I am now!" "I have arrived. I am home." "I am just right."* Not perfect. Not without challenges and opportunities. Not without confusions, aches and pains, but full, real, and authentically who we are.

The key to knowing—not to believing, but to knowing—that the best is yet to come is not found in having or doing more. Instead, as poet Mark Nepo reminds us: *"The truth is that one experience taken to heart will satisfy our hunger to be loved [admired, recognized, remembered] by everyone."*

Imagine that! Enough…satisfaction…completeness! Not someday, but today. Fulfillment as close as this breath, and our willingness to be present and to experience and explore this moment! Wholeness, individuation, enlightenment, or whatever each of us calls the state of grace and bliss we seek, available not by consuming all of the cherries but by savoring the one we are currently eating, not by hoping or wishing to be somewhere, or someone, different, but by diving fully into this ocean of now and simply and lovingly uncovering and expressing who we are born to be. Then we can sing our notes in the precious song of life in a way that only we can.

About the Authors

Photo by Lisa Law

George and Sedena Cappannelli are authors, consultants, speakers, and cofounders of AgeNation, a digital media company and social enterprise, and The Age of Empowerment, a 501(c)(3) serving vulnerable sections of our aging population.

They are experts on individual, organizational, and societal change, with an outstanding track record serving hundreds of thousands of individuals and hundreds of the world's leading organizations in both the private and public sectors.

George and Sedena are hosts on two national radio talk shows, *AgeNation Radio Magazine* and *Conversations with the Wisdom Keepers*. George is also an Emmy Award–winning film and television producer and director, has been privileged to work with a number of world leaders, and is an award-winning sculptor. Sedena, a long-time member of the Screen Actors Guild, has appeared in numerous films, television programs, and theatrical productions. Her new Personal Energy Program (PEP) DVD and book introduce a series of groundbreaking wellness and deaging processes.

Together, George and Sedena are coauthors of three previous books: *Do Not Go Quietly: A Guide to Living Consciously and Aging Wisely for People Who Weren't Born Yesterday*; *Say Yes to Change: 25 Keys to Making Change Work for You*; and *Authenticity: Simple Strategies for Greater Meaning and Purpose at Work and at Home.*

They are also cofounders of AgeNation, the company whose mission is to provide information, inspiration, education, products and services, and opportunities for community and engagement for people who weren't born yesterday, a constituency that will soon be 150 million strong with many things still to learn, much to contribute, and the opportunity to make things right with themselves and others.

To learn more, visit **www.agenation.com.**

About *Do Not Go Quietly*

If you like *The Best Is Yet to Be: How to Age Wisely and Fall in Love with Your Life...Again*, you'll also like *Do Not Go Quietly: A Guide to Living Consciously and Aging Wisely for People Who Weren't Born Yesterday*.

Winner of nine national book awards and recommended by Hay House as one of the "Top 15 Must-Read Books of 2014," *Do Not Go Quietly* reminds us that we are never too old or too young to live our dreams, remember the power and resources we have to meet the challenges and opportunities that lie ahead, and to make right our relationships with ourselves and others.

It is an inspiring call to action and a guide to a life of greater meaning and purpose for Gen Xers, Boomers, and Elders, as well as younger people who want to better prepare for the road ahead.

Practical, accessible, and loaded with thousands of recommendations and hundreds of inspiring stories and quotes, *Do Not Go Quietly* has been called "profound, practical, and deeply useful…a guide to the genius and capacities inherent in the second half of life," by bestselling author and wise woman Jean Houston.

New Thought leader Michael Beckwith says, "*Do Not Go Quietly* offers invaluable insights into what is an increasingly valuable subject of our time and our collective future."

Do Not Go Quietly is available at Amazon, Barnes & Noble, and bookstores everywhere. Visit **www.donotgoquietlythebook.com** for free downloads, guided imagery audios, and much more.